Proof Positive

Developing Significant Volunteer Recordkeeping Systems

21st Century Edition

Susan J. Ellis

Katherine Noyes Campbell

Proof Positive: Developing Significant Volunteer Recordkeeping Systems,
21st Century Edition
Copyright ©2003 by Energize, Inc.
5450 Wissahickon Avenue
Philadelphia, PA 19144
www.energizeinc.com

ISBN 0-940576-29-5, revised edition, 2003—electronic
ISBN 0-940576-37-6, revised edition, 2003—print

This is a revision of the 1990 edition of *Proof Positive*
ISBN *0-940576-10-4*
Library of Congress Catalog Number 90-82887

PRINTED IN THE UNITED STATES OF AMERICA

Contents

Before You Begin (1980, 1990, 2003) i

1 THINKING IT THROUGH 1

2 THE CORE VOLUNTEER TRACKING SYSTEM 5

3 TIME AND ACTIVITY RECORDS 17

4 DESIGN, MANAGEMENT AND UPKEEP 33

5 POWERFUL REPORTING 39

6 PLUNGING IN 47

Appendix: If you are still using paper... 49

Index 67

Before You Begin...

PREFACE TO THE ORIGINAL EDITION, 1980

We feel a kinship with all readers of this book because we, too, have struggled with the complexities of designing and maintaining records on volunteer programs. The thoughts and suggestions on the following pages are based on our own experience and on what we have seen done by many other volunteer program directors. We offer these to you because they have been tested in many types of programs and they work!

The material here will make the most sense if you read it through in order, since we try to present a sequential examination of recordkeeping principles. Because every volunteer program is unique, we have not tried to create a single, universal record-keeping design. Rather, we present the basic elements of a recordkeeping system and guidelines for developing your own version of the forms and procedures described. Although we have provided some sample forms as illustrations, our goal was to give you the practical, how-to information necessary to adapt and create a system that is right for you.

We hope you will find *Proof Positive* useful whether you are new to volunteer administration or a veteran. Please note that we use the word "program" as a general term to describe what volunteers are doing in the wide variety of agencies and organizations you represent. In the last section we give some ideas for implementing these recordkeeping practices, especially if you want to make changes in an already-existing system. The important thing to remember is that recordkeeping does not have to be drudgery and can become a satisfying (or even fun!) part of your job.

Susan J. Ellis and Katherine H. Noyes
Philadelphia 1980

TEN YEARS LATER (1990)...

In re-examining this book a decade after it was first published, we are pleased that so much of it remains pertinent. We are grateful to readers of the original edition for their comments and suggestions, many of which led to the revisions we have made in the following pages.

Technology has caught up with us and so *Proof Positive* now contains a chapter on computers. But a computer is only a tool for doing things faster and with less duplication. You still need a basic system for gathering data and a goal for how you will use it. That is why all the elements of the manual recordkeeping system we present in this book remain relevant even if you have a computer from the beginning of your program. If you later acquire a computer, having organized manual records will permit you to transfer easily to the electronic age.

Susan J. Ellis and Katherine H. Noyes
Philadelphia 1990

IN 2003...

In 1990 we were on the cutting edge by even acknowledging the new availability of desktop computers. The world has changed! In 2003, most volunteer offices maintain records electronically and there are various software programs designed specifically for tracking volunteer management data. There are even Internet options for keeping records online.

But computers still cannot get off the desk and gather data independently! So to make the most of new technology, you still need to:

1. Know what you want and how you'll use and report on the data.

2. Be organized.

3. Have effective data gathering procedures.

That's why this book remains on target! Read on...

Susan J. Ellis and Katherine Noyes Campbell
Philadelphia 2003

1 Thinking It Through

☑ *Do you think of recordkeeping as boring, time-consuming, and unrelated to the more rewarding aspects of day-to-day work with volunteers?*

☑ *Do you gather and report only the minimum amount of data required by "higher-ups"?*

☑ *How often do you re-examine and redesign your forms and procedures?*

☑ *How often do you throw out forms that have lost their value?*

☑ *Are you making full use of the features in your volunteer management software program?*

In answering these questions, recognize that you control your recordkeeping system and that you can mold it to do whatever you need it to. Recordkeeping only seems a waste of time if it is an end unto itself. Therefore you must integrate this responsibility into the other aspects of program management. Start by identifying the variety of uses to which you can put the data collected. Look at the following list and determine which uses are important to you (and add others not mentioned, of course):

- To keep you in touch with what's going on
- To evaluate program effectiveness
- To document your own achievements
- To document volunteer achievements
- To justify program expansion
- To provide information for public relations/media contacts
- To convince resistant salaried staff of the worth of volunteers
- To develop a program history
- To recognize the work of volunteers
- To identify gaps in service
- To support volunteers' income tax returns, job resumes, college applications, insurance claims, etc.
- To be accountable
- To demonstrate "community support"
- To use as in-kind match in funding proposals
- To identify volunteer and employee training needs

✦ To identify your personal training needs

✦ To determine age, race, and other characteristics of all the volunteers

✦ To aid in long-range planning

✦ To get information to use in recruitment

Does your present recordkeeping system allow you to do all the things you selected above? If not, the time has come to reassess and redesign your methods.

Begin with this basic principle:

A good recordkeeping system is a SYSTEM.

All forms, procedures and records must interlock and logically relate to one another. When a new need for information arises, new data collecting methods must be designed to mesh with the existing system.

COMPUTERIZED VOLUNTEER RECORDS

When we wrote the first edition of this book in 1980, computers were practically non-existent in volunteer resources offices. By the time of the second edition in 1990, we had to add a whole chapter on computers[1], but the focus was on determining if you needed a computer and what to look for in a software program. Fast forward to 2003! Today we are going to make the following assumptions:

1. The volunteer resources office has a desktop or laptop computer available to maintain volunteer records.

2. You have either purchased one of the various commercial volunteer management software programs or have the ability to create a database that will work for your needs.

If these assumptions are wrong and you are still working completely on paper, we aren't abandoning you! Simply go to the Appendix of this book and you can read everything we told people to do in the earlier editions. Believe it or not, the old-fashioned system will still work for you.

In fact, you might want to browse the Appendix even if you are computerized. Some of the system may seem hopelessly outdated to you because of its discussion of such quaint tools as paper index cards. But, again, the basic concepts of what information you need about volunteers and how you need to keep current—beyond an "address list"—are as important to define in the 21st century as they were when recordkeeping was done on parchment with quill pens!

Selecting Software

Your first decision will be whether to purchase one of the available volunteer management software programs, integrate your records with existing software used in your organization for other data such as tracking donations or memberships, or design your own software (from scratch or adapting a generic database program such as Microsoft Access™). The best idea is to research exactly what the packaged programs do and how much flexibility they provide for you to add data unique to your needs. Talk to other volunteer program managers actually using the product. Make a list of what you absolutely must be able to do and what would be nice to do, but not essential. Then talk to the distributor of the program and see how your list matches the software's capabilities.

Once you have your software installed, you are ready to begin computerizing your volunteer information system. One of the first things you will need to do is record basic data on each active volunteer and about the various assignments volunteers fill. That's what the next few chapters will discuss.

While being able to store all the information about your volunteer program is a benefit of a computer, your first task is to figure out what information is really important—useful to you as a manager—and what you need to know.

For example, if you often search for volunteers to come in at short notice, it may be important to store the days and times a volunteer is willing to serve. If you want to monitor the turnover rate in a particular assignment or unit, then you must somehow record the starting and ending dates of all assigned volunteers.

Everything described in *Proof Positive* can be entered into a computer, including the original manual system now shown in the Appendix. That manual system frequently records data in columns or boxes. These correspond to the computer concept of "fields": specific units of information that are uniform, comparable, and can be sorted and organized.

One more note about software: be sure your database is able to retain the history of your volunteer program. When you mark a volunteer as "inactive," the computer should still be able to retrieve information about that volunteer when you ask for reports that go back in time—while leaving that inactive volunteer off any list of current volunteers. This is a good test of what your proposed software can do.

A Word on Donated Computers

If you are in a nonprofit organization, you may be able to obtain a donated computer system from a business or even an individual. Though this may be a great opportunity, if the donated system does not run the right type of software for your needs, you could end up wasting a lot of time.

If you can still get the right kind of software for the donated equipment, you may face other problems. Is the equipment in good condition? Who can fix it if something goes wrong? Are any warranties or maintenance agreements still in effect? In the early days of personal computers there were many brands made by companies that are no longer in existence. If the donated machine is one of these "orphaned" computers, is there someone who can still support (i.e., service, answer questions about, provide supplies for) the equipment?

It helps to understand the possible concerns before you accept donated computer equipment. But there are plenty of good, reliable computers out there that can continue to provide much service, so a donation may be the best way for you to obtain a computer at minimum expense. It does not make much difference what brand of computer you get as long as you know that you will have the necessary software to make it useful for you.

GETTING THE MOST FROM YOUR COMPUTER

In the beginning you will find that the computer may take more of your time, instead of saving you time. This is to be expected if you are making the conversion from a manual system to a computerized one. In order for the computer to become a time-saver, you must first prime it with data. As you enter more and more information into the computer, and as your experience grows, you will begin to see the benefits of the computer.

Once your data is in the computer, you can begin to do the things that make use of the incredibly rapid sorting capability of the machine. Here are some of the ways you can make the most of your records (providing your software allows you to do these):

- When a flu outbreak causes ten volunteers to miss their scheduled day, you can generate a list, with phone numbers, of any other volunteers who said they might be available on short notice. (Again, this presupposes you *asked* all volunteers whether they might be called and then *recorded* their answers—the computer only contains information you put into it!).

- Before your annual recognition event, you can generate a list of volunteers in order of their starting date with the program—listing the most veteran volunteers first.

- You can search for any volunteer who has not been active for more than 30 days and follow up to learn why.

- On a weekly basis you can make a list of any unfilled volunteer assignments—by unit, by date of request, or by any other criterion.

- You can send a letter to all people who left their volunteer assignment in the last six months, asking them for feedback on their experience in your organization.

- As often as you want, you can issue a report to each department, unit, committee chair, or anyone else about the volunteers assigned to them.

Every one of these examples could be done manually, equally well. But the computer can do the work in a fraction of the time it would take to do it with paper forms and a typewriter. You are more likely to use your data when you can access it simply and quickly.

Everything begins with your ability to describe what you need from the computer.

---

[1]Continuing thanks to Bruce W. Bechtold, whose chapter on computerization in the 1990 edition of this book was so cutting-edge then that sections of it are still relevant now and are adapted here.

2 The Core Volunteer Tracking System

No matter what kind of volunteer program you lead, there is a core of information which your recordkeeping system must provide. This is the data that tells you who is volunteering and for what.

APPLICATION FORM

A prospective volunteer application form is necessary for two reasons: to assist in your interview and screening process; and to document basic information about individual volunteers. The form should be seen as a tool to be used as a starting point in an interview. Whereas volunteer programs need to ask for some personal data from potential volunteers, there is no real reason to follow the paid employment application model in designing your form. The most common mistake made in designing application forms is to ask too much in writing that tells you too little about the potential volunteer.

When was the last time you took a good look at the application form you ask prospective volunteers to complete? It's easy to grow accustomed to a tried-and-true form, especially one that we use almost daily. But find a moment to review it just to make sure it is doing its job as effectively as possible.

As well as assessing if the form gives you the data you need, consider its tone. What does the application convey to a prospective volunteer about what's important to your organization? What might a potential volunteer learn about you from completing this form? Are the questions very formal or more colloquial? Does there seem to be interest in who the applicant is as a person beyond the facts of his/her credentials? Do you want to know about past volunteering as well as about past paid employment? What level of education or literacy is implied by the vocabulary in your questions or the number of essay answers expected? If you aren't sure what tone your application conveys, ask some volunteers who have completed it recently. Then consider how you might rephrase or add questions that are more welcoming.

Regardless of how you design your form, the following are elements to include on a basic application:

Element	Considerations
Title of Form	The word "application" does not have to appear on the top of the form, since it can seem unnecessarily formal or even threatening to some individuals. Other options are *Prospective Volunteer Profile* or *Volunteer Candidate Information.*
Date	It is useful for follow up and filing purposes to have the date of the application visible at the top of the form.
Name, Address, Telephone Number(s)	Obviously this is important information, but ask for both "permanent" and "temporary" addresses (such as would be applicable to some student volunteers). Also, do you need "day" and "evening" telephone numbers?
E-mail Address	It is vital to ask for e-mail address because, as time goes on, this is likely to be the primary way you will communicate with volunteers. You may need to ask for personal and business e-mail address—and which the volunteer prefers you to use. [*Note*: If your current application form does not include a line for e-mail now, you don't have to throw out a ream of printed forms. Have a rubber stamp made that says: "E-mail address:_____" and stamp it at the top of every application. Really.]
Age, Sex, Race, Marital Status	These items may or may not be important to your assessment of a potential volunteer. Legally, you must have a specific purpose in asking for this information on a screening application—otherwise volunteers must be given the same civil rights protection as are candidates for employment. This means such information cannot be used for screening purposes, but once you have accepted a person as a volunteer, you may ask such demographic profile data for your records.

Element	Considerations
Education	Think about exactly what you most want to know about the applicant's education. Do dates of graduation matter? Could this section of your form discourage a prospective volunteer without a formal degree? You could ask an open-ended question here, such as "describe any training you have had that relates to our type of organization" or "what was your most recent formal education?"
Relevant Experience	Be sure to indicate your interest in *both* salaried and volunteer work experience. While you may want to know the applicant's present occupation, do you need a lot of detail about present and past employers?
Interests and Skills	You can uncover this information in a number of ways. Realize that just because a person has a skill does not mean he or she necessarily wants to use it on your behalf. So ask for this information in relation to willingness to share the talent. Both open-ended and checklist questions can work well. If you select the checklist format, be sure that volunteer assignments really exist for all the skills listed, or else you are raising false expectations.
Availability	This is information that will probably change often. So you might want to note the person's possible schedule elsewhere rather than on the application form which will be kept as a permanent record.
Emergency Contact	It is a good idea to ask for the name, telephone number, and relationship to the applicant of a person to notify in case of emergency.
Transportation Needs, Health Restrictions, Parental Permission, Other Affiliations, Reason for Applying, etc.	These—and other types of information— might be of help to you in screening and assigning a new volunteer. Select *only* those of real value to you.

Element	Considerations
References	State that, by completing this portion of the form, the applicant is giving you permission to contact these people. It's best to ask for references only if you are truly going to follow up and contact them.
"Office Only" Notes	At the bottom or on the back of the application form leave space in which to jot down your notes during or after the interview, as well as places for indicating "final decision," "assignment," starting date," etc.
Initial Commitment	It is extremely useful to write down the duration of the initial commitment of service offered by a new volunteer. If you note that a person intends to volunteer for approximately one year, you can later evaluate your retention success or failure.

The following two pages show a sample volunteer application form, using some of the elements as described. As always, adapt this form for your specific needs.

If the applicant does not become a volunteer, the application form should be kept as a record of the interview. This documents time spent by you and interest shown in the program. It might also demonstrate your concern for adequate screening. Keep non-activated applications in a special folder or binder, chronologically.

If the applicant does become a volunteer, you are ready to begin a permanent record of that person's service, using the volunteer tracking system.

PROSPECTIVE VOLUNTEER PROFILE SHEET

Date: _____

Name: _____

(last)   (first)   (m.i.)

Contact Address: _____

_____

(Is this address: ___home? ___business? __temporary?)
If your permanent address is different from the one above, please write it on the reverse of this form.

Day Telephone:_____ Evening Telephone_____

E-mail address:_____ (__home? __work?)
How would you prefer being contacted? __ phone __ e-mail/ __day __evening

Present Occupation:_____

Employer or School:_____

Please describe any paid or volunteer work experience you have had that might relate to your interest in volunteering here:

What training or formal education have you had that might help you volunteer with us?

Do you have any physical limitations on the type of work you could do here?

Interests/Skills   The following are some of the skills needed for our volunteer assignments. Place a "C" next to all of those that you <u>can do</u> (and are willing to do!) and an "L" next to any you might <u>like to learn</u>.

_____Drawing/Painting   _____Calligraphy
_____Newsletter article writing   _____Photography
_____Computer data entry   _____Party planning
_____Coaching sports   _____Playing an instrument
_____Which?_____   Which?_____
_____Receptionist work   _____Leading tours
_____Working with small children   _____Working with seniors

What other skills or interests do you have that you'd like to use in your volunteering?

Availability How many hours per week do you wish to
              volunteer?_____

              If you do not want a weekly schedule, what is
              your preference?_____

Please use the grid below to show your current availability to volunteer. Mark only those times that you most prefer.

	Monday	Tuesday	Wednesday	Thursday	Friday	Saturday
Morning						
Afternoon						
Evening						

How long would you like your initial commitment to be with us?
___six months   ___one year   ___other:_____

Emergency
Contact:_____

For Office Use Only   Date of Interview:
                                   Interviewer:

Notes: Action:

VOLUNTEER TRACKING SYSTEM

A basic volunteer recordkeeping system must allow you to have the following information easily available at all times:

- exactly who is volunteering now, and for what;
- basic facts on each volunteer, past and present;
- the history of every volunteer assignment in the program (who filled what position and which assignments have vacancies to be filled);
- comparative data on past and present volunteers.

In the old paper system, we had three basic components: Volunteer Fact Cards, Volunteer Folders, and a Master Log. If you are going to keep records manually, go to the Appendix and read the instructions there in detail.

Using a computer, we now must have a Volunteer Data Record and an Assignment Record. But we still need a file cabinet because we're going to need Volunteer Folders, too.

Before you put fingers to keyboard, think through what you are most likely to want to know about volunteers on a regular basis, what information you need to store but won't necessarily look at often, and how you expect to use the system. This is much, much more than a complicated "mailing list." This is data you will actually use in managing the volunteer program. For example, consider questions such as:

- ☑ Do you need to contact volunteers on a daily or weekly basis?
- ☑ Do you make contact by phone? E-mail? Postal mail?
- ☑ Are you likely to want to search often for such things as special skills, schedule availability, or other data? What do you want to store vs. what do you want as searchable?
- ☑ Will you want to enter dates for such things as training or recognition received, or will a simple check-off do?
- ☑ How likely are you to want to write notes into the record? About what?
- ☑ Who will enter the data into the system—and make decisions about what to say and where to put data?
- ☑ How many people will access the records and for what purpose?

All of these questions and others have an impact on how you should design your system. This is one reason there is no one-size-fits-all answer to recordkeeping. Even an off-the-shelf software program will give you opportunities to modify fields, format screens, and use your own vocabulary to make the program yours.

Volunteer Data Record

The source of the information you will initially enter into each volunteer data record is, of course, the volunteer application form and notes that you made during the interview. The way that you organize the data is what's important. Some pointers (though you may be limited by the flexibility of the software you are using):

1. **Don't clutter the main screen with information you rarely use.** The beauty of computers is that a tremendous amount of information can be stored and accessed by simple "clicks" to bring up additional screens. The main screen should have the information you are most likely to need most often. Obviously this includes name, address, phone, e-mail, and current assignment.

2. **Make the fields long enough.** A "field" is the space in which you enter specific units of information that are uniform, comparable, and can be sorted and organized. Think of it like a box or line on a paper form. Depending on how a specific piece of information will later be used by the software, you may have fields ranging from an area allowing you to enter only one character to a limitless area for notes. Nothing is more frustrating than discovering your program won't allow you to enter a very long name, address or other information. Be alert to such needs as space for multi-line business addresses and space for data you may want to add in the future (you don't have to use it now, but you will be endlessly grateful later if you thought ahead).

3. **Allow for alternatives.** Because volunteer programs value diversity, you will quickly find that you need to keep more information on some volunteers than on others. For example, if someone volunteers both as an individual and with a regularly-scheduled group, you will want the Volunteer Data Record to accommodate that. As we noted on the application, some people will have "permanent" and "temporary" addresses. For young volunteers, you may want to add in contact information about their parents, or possibly about the teacher who referred the class to you. Give yourself fields for additional addresses, multiple sources, etc.

4. **Make as much data as possible "searchable."** We cannot give a full tutorial on databases here, but it is helpful to understand some of the basics of how information is retrieved or sorted by a computer. The two major searches (and this is very simplified) are by field and by keyword. The easiest way to explain the difference is to think about a person's name. Let's say you have a volunteer named Abraham Lincoln. Your choices for entering this data on screen would be:

2 fields or boxes, one for first and one for last name:

Abraham	Lincoln

or...

1 larger field or box, in which you write the full name:

Abraham Lincoln

When you have created discrete fields for each piece of information as in the first example, the software program can sort easily—by first name, last name, or by any other field. The second example, however, poses a harder challenge to the software. It "sees" all the characters as one field. Unless you have software that is capable of going into every field and searching for keywords, Abraham Lincoln may only be searchable by his first name. If you enter it last name first like this...

Lincoln, Abraham

...then the system will "see" the data as starting with L. Punctuation matters, too. Some software programs can recognize words that are separated by commas.

For something like a name, the issue may seem simple. But now consider information such as a volunteer's list of skills. If you enter the data into a text box all jumbled together like this...

```
calligraphy, can drive and has license,
speaks Spanish
```

...make sure your software can retrieve each skill from within the text. On the other hand, if you enter the data separately as below, you know that you can definitely search by field:

```
calligraphy        driver            license

Spanish
```

Clearly, you want to be able to generate as many fields as you need. If you do this well, later you will be able to sort all the files for "who can speak Spanish?" or any other skills, almost instantly.

It is also possible to create codes for some bits of information. This allows you to use alphanumeric "shorthand" for things such as skills. But then you need a glossary of codes either available within the database or near the computer, or else you will never remember that "C1" is the code for "calligraphy"!

5. **Start and keep a history of milestones.** The application form will give you personal data, but the Volunteer Data Record is also where you will want to track various interaction with the volunteer over time. Some types of data that you may want to record as an ongoing history:

   ✦ Special work done outside a regular assignment (what, dates)
   ✦ Training received (session names, dates)
   ✦ Recognition received (dates, award levels reached)

Depending on your setting, you may also want to track such things as:

   ✦ Background check completed
   ✦ Parental permission received
   ✦ Health screenings passed
   ✦ Uniform received
   ✦ Volunteer manual received (and then updates)

6. **Leave room for notes.** Apart from personal data that you need for every volunteer and things that you may want to search for, the Volunteer Data Record is also where you will want to record comments, notes on important conversations, and other individualized material.

7. **Record multiple assignments.** Be sure you have the capability to enter more than one assignment at a time for volunteers who do several things. It is important to be able to designate which of the current assignments is the primary one for that volunteer. This will matter later when you generate program statistics. Each volunteer will be counted in the grand total of volunteers through his or her primary assignment, though will be reflected (but not counted twice) in each multiple role as well (see pages 40-42).

8. **Credit completed commitments.** As noted in the discussion of application form information, you should be asking how long a volunteer expects her or his initial commitment to be. Only if you know how long a volunteer planned to stay, can you assess what your "retention" rate is. Retention is best defined as "a volunteer remaining in an assignment for at least the length of time promised." So create a field in the Volunteer Data Record for initial commitment. When the time comes that this volunteer leaves, it is obvious by comparing the termination date to the commitment promised whether or not "retention" occurred. Your software should let you generate a report of all the people who left during the year and which stayed exactly as long as promised, which left earlier, and which remained with you for much longer than originally anticipated.

Apart from personal data, the Volunteer Record is where you will enter all assignments the volunteer accepts (by title, unit or supervisor, and dates) and other supporting details you need (and this may vary from assignment to assignment).

Volunteer Assignment Record

This is one of the features that distinguishes a true volunteer management software program from a generic database. It is not enough to be able to identify, sort, and search volunteers by their names, skills, or other personal data. You have to be able to connect each person to the assignments s/he is carrying now and has held in the past. Further, you need to be able to search and report by assignment. At any given time, you need to know at least:

- What volunteer assignments are currently being filled.
- Who is serving in each assignment now.
- Who served in that assignment on X date.
- Which assignments have vacancies.
- What the turnover is in each assignment.
- Who is carrying more than one assignment.

A decent software program should allow you to store complete volunteer position descriptions. This is a marvelous feature because you can keep each one completely current and print it out with a click of a button when you are interviewing a prospective candidate for that volunteer role.

Along with each volunteer position description, you need supporting information, including:

- Where does this work take place physically? (with all the location details)
- Who is the supervisor or staff liaison? (with all contact information)
- When was the position created and by whom? When was it last updated?
- Generally, when are volunteers needed to do this work? (days, times)
- As of today, when are volunteers needed to do this work? (vacancies in the schedule)
- How many volunteers can be accommodated at one time?
- Can groups as well as individuals do this?
- What is the orientation and training plan for this position?

Create fields for all these pieces of information and any others relevant to each position. You can develop similar files for larger projects or events.

This data is for your use in daily program management. It should give you the details you need to share with volunteers, to support supervisory staff, and to make the best decisions.

Who Is Doing What?

The manual system described in the Appendix recommends a "Master Log" to track which volunteers are in which assignments. Computers remove the need for a such a Log, because you will gather the same information automatically through your software's reporting function.

As soon as you enter an assignment into the individual Volunteer Data Record, the software will link that field with the Assignment Record (this is a simplistic way of describing the technology). When you are in the Volunteer Assignment Record, you should be able to click to a list of who is filling the role now—with any parameters you wish, such as who filled it last month. In addition, you can ask the system to give you names only, or names and e-mail addresses, or names and starting dates—whatever information you want at that minute for your management needs.

It is common for some volunteers to fill more than one assignment at a time. The Individual Volunteer Data Record can easily capture all the roles. But be sure that the software does not "double count" multi-tasking volunteers. It's important to be able to generate an accurate list of which volunteers are active in any given assignment, yet also to get an accurate count of how many individuals are on board regardless of assignment(s). See more about this in chapter 5 on reporting.

Similarly, when it comes time to write your monthly or annual report, you can set up your data sort to provide all sorts of vital evidence of the hard work of volunteers during the period.

We said this before but it is worth saying again: It is extremely important for the system to maintain records on past volunteers as well as on current ones, and on assignments held in the past by volunteers who have moved on to new work with you. You need to search by date for purposes of recognition, evaluation, recruitment, and other planning. This may even be needed to support an insurance claim or tax deduction, even after several years have passed.

Volunteer Folders

The Volunteer Folder is where you place everything about the volunteer that is not in the Data Record. There should be a Folder for every volunteer, into which you immediately place the application form. As time goes by, you will add reference letters, parental permission slips, evaluation forms, recommendations, reports, and correspondence relating to that individual.

You can use color coding to identify certain subgroups (e.g., students receiving academic credit for their service), if you feel it is important to your use of the file. It rarely is.

File Volunteer Folders according to "active" and "terminated" status, alphabetically within each section.

3 Time and Activity Records

Now you have a record of who the volunteers are and how to contact them, as well as details about the assignments they fill. But this information is static. It hardly reflects the true contributions that volunteers make to your organization every day. That's why you need to capture what volunteers do and accomplish.

TALLYING VOLUNTEER HOURS

For better or for worse, tallies of volunteer hours served are almost universally requested as a primary indicator of the contribution of volunteers to an organization or community (we'll give you additional indicators later in this chapter). Documenting hours sounds straightforward, but can become a headache as programs grow in size and complexity. The goal, therefore, is to develop a method of collecting this data that is accurate and workable. Variables to consider in designing forms and procedures include:

- *The location of volunteer service:* Do all or some volunteers actually work on-site in an organizational office/facility? Do all or some volunteers work at scattered sites, or on their own?

- *Hidden time:* Are volunteers spending additional time preparing for their volunteer assignment or doing outside things related to the organization? Is such service being effectively documented?

- *Your needs vs. other needs:* Does your facility require a daily record of who was in the building? How often do you want to compile tallies of hours for both individual volunteers and the program as a whole?

Note that there is a distinct difference between the need to document the ongoing service record of each volunteer and the value of knowing how many and which volunteers serve on a given day or during a given month. You may want to do both, but the rationales are different. The former is part of your necessary supervision, recognition, and support of volunteers as individuals. The latter provides management information to help you in program and space scheduling, planning, and paid staff relations, as well as providing a legal record for the agency.

There are many models of documenting time being used successfully in countless programs. If you have a system that works for you, that's great. However, if you have no system yet or are dissatisfied with what you are now doing, consider the following possibilities.

INDIVIDUAL TIME REPORTS

An Individual Time Report is a one-page form—on paper or electronic—designed to capture the cumulative hours contributed by each volunteer during a specific period of time. This is one instance in which the procedure you develop for completing and collecting the Time Reports is as important as the form itself.

If you are working in a large organization, you may be able to purchase software that allows every volunteer to log into the computer each time they come on site, even from different locations. Then they record their attendance directly into the system and you do not need to handle a paper trail. There are even touch-screen "kiosks" on the market that allow this to be done quickly, though expensively.

Most agencies rely on individually-submitted time reports. Any size organization can develop an e-mail reporting system to do exactly what a paper format does.

The following are elements you might include on a time report:

Element	Considerations
Name of Volunteer and Assignment	Obviously this information is needed at the very top of the page.
Period Covered	There should be a space for noting the "Week of_____" or the "Month of _____" or whatever period of time you have designated.
Date	For each day on which the volunteer works, an entry will be made.
Hours	This can either be a column or space for "total hours" that day, or be a more detailed breakdown such as: In /Out for Meal/In from Meal/Out This information can be filled in exactly or rounded off to the nearest quarter or half hour.
Location	You might want to know where the time was spent: "office," "field," "client's home," "own home," etc.

Element	Considerations
Summary of Activities	You might want to create a wide column or space in which a volunteer can note the type of activity (or highlights) handled on each date recorded. If you want to know the names of the clients/participants with whom the volunteer spent time, ask for that to be included here. Encourage volunteers to log time spent *preparing* for volunteer work as well as time on site. Such a record not only gives you a quick overview of how volunteers are being utilized, but also gives the volunteer a sort of progress diary of his or her involvement.
Questions, Problems, or Suggestions	Another possible column or area could be for noting questions or problems needing supervisory attention. But if volunteers write things into this area, be sure that you (or someone) respond!
Total Hours	At the bottom of the form, indicate a space for totaling the hours recorded on the sheet.
Supervisor's Signature	You might find it useful to have the volunteer's immediate supervisor (paid or volunteer) sign the form after reviewing it. This is the person most likely to notice if the volunteer did not record all time contributed in that period and can follow up to complete the data.

Train all volunteers to complete their Individual Time Report every day they work for you. You must continually emphasize the importance of this quick task, and explain its value to the volunteer. Points to stress are:

🖝 having an accurate record of days and times served supports a volunteer's IRS forms and insurance claims, and documents work experience for resumes;

🖝 the volunteer doubles his or her contribution to the organization by keeping accurate time records that can later be converted into in-kind matching funds for a variety of grants;

🖝 keeping track of hours and activities leads to appropriate recognition.

If you set forth the firm expectation that completing Time Reports is part of a volunteer's job, you will get results. Do not let those few individuals who are lax in completing the forms get away with it. Follow up and prove you read them!

Individual Time Report

Month, Yr_____

Name_____ Assignment_____

Date	Summary of Activities	Total Time (S/F)	Comments/Questions

Remeber to show the time on site (S)

and in the field (F) Total for Mo.:

Response	Response	Response
From: Date:	From: Date:	From: Date:

© 2003 Energize, Inc.

Estimating Time Spent

There are times when it is hard to pinpoint exact number of hours served. It is legitimate to estimate the average time for a particular volunteer task and to use that in a time tally. For example, taking a child to the movies might be "counted" as 4 hours of service (in the knowledge that sometimes this activity takes more or less time, balancing your estimate). See page 23 for more on this way to record volunteer work not conducive to "signing in."

Keeping Time Reports in View

Where you physically place the Individual Time Reports has a great deal to do with how well they are completed. Options include:

1. Individual "mail slots" for each volunteer: This works for smaller programs in which volunteers work on site. Make sure the forms are kept in each slot and are collected and replaced by your office each month (or week) on time. You might want to print the form on brightly colored paper so that it will always be visible in the slot, regardless of other mail or messages.

2. A looseleaf notebook containing all Individual Time Reports in alphabetical order. This can either be kept as one notebook in a central location or as several notebooks placed at the main work sites for volunteers. Again it is imperative that the sheets are collected and replaced on time.

When you collect the Individual Time Reports each month or week, see that each volunteer's "total" of hours served is entered into the computer system or, if you are working manually, on the Individual Work Record in that volunteer's Folder (see Appendix). For your program reporting needs, you compile whatever totals you wish, e.g., number of hours given to each assignment, number of hours given per site, etc. Then you file the entire set of Individual Time Reports for a given period together in a folder and file each folder in chronological order.

For volunteers holding more than one assignment, you can either make up two separate Time Reports (noting on each sheet that it is part of a set), or you can use the one form and instruct the volunteer to record which assignment he or she was carrying on which date. Then you can total the hours for each assignment separately on the same sheet.

A sample Individual Time Report, incorporating many of the elements just suggested, appears on the previous page. Suggestions for using e-mail reporting end this chapter.

ON-SITE ATTENDANCE FORMS

Those of you who want to be aware of which volunteers are on site on a daily basis—and do not have the sophisticated computer program allowing automatic entry of data at "point of service" by each volunteer—must utilize an additional form. Options include:

Daily Sign-In Sheet: This is not meant to replace the Individual Time Reports because that would require the immense task of finding and transferring all data on individual volunteers from up to 31 sheets per month. Rather, it should be a simple form requiring a volunteer to sign in as proof of attendance that day. The volunteer logs hours, other notes about activities or progress, etc. on his or her Individual Time Report, kept near the Sign-In Sheet. Do not ask volunteers to repeat hours on both forms. This would be unnecessary duplication. Keep in mind that this system requires storage of up to 31 lists per month. Do you want this?

Monthly Grid: An easier and more useful method would be to design a monthly grid such as the one below.

You write all the volunteers' names in the left column at the start of the month, adding new volunteers as necessary. You can make up a grid for each assignment. Happily, your computer system should be able to generate the grid for you at the start of each period—if your entries are up to date. The grid can be enlarged and posted on a wall.

Each volunteer places a check mark in the appropriate date column, next to his or her name, when reporting to work. The volunteer also completes the Individual Time Report, kept near the grid. Or, you can eliminate the separate Time Report by asking each volunteer to enter the total hours served each day in the correct box.

This method allows you to count volunteers in attendance each day as well as for the entire month. At a glance, you see attendance patterns, both for individual volunteers and for the program as a whole. You can cross check the accuracy of the Individual Time Reports by making sure that every volunteer has logged hours for each day checked on the grid. If volunteers are recording their hours directly onto the grid, adding across on each line gives you each volunteer's monthly total of hours, while adding down tells you the number of hours contributed each day by all volunteers in attendance.

Month:																																
Names of Volunteers	1	2	3	4	5	6	7	8	9	10	11	12	13	14	15	16	17	18	19	20	21	22	23	24	25	26	27	28	29	30	31	total
Daily Totals:																																

OFF-SITE VOLUNTEERS

Much of this discussion on how to record volunteer hours focuses on volunteers who serve in your facility, coming on site to do their work. But many volunteer assignments do not require this sort of physical base and are done off-site instead, in "the field." A growing number of agencies also recruit volunteers to handle virtual assignments, in which the service is done online through the Internet, at whatever location or time the volunteer chooses. This means that you, as program leader, do not see volunteers while they are working and can only capture their contributions by relying on them to report back to you.

It is possible to use the same time or progress reports for off-site volunteers as for on-site ones, but ask that the forms be e-mailed or postal mailed in to you on a monthly basis. For those without a computer, supply a stamped, self-addressed envelope. For those who elect to use e-mail, send the e-mail form a few days before the report is due back to you.

Because many programs have found it difficult to get 100% cooperation in returning this type of form, another option is to ask off-site volunteers to keep track in any way they wish of the days and hours they are serving. Then recruit one or more in-office volunteers who enjoy recordkeeping and assign them to *telephone* the off-site volunteers, on a regular schedule, to obtain the information. The volunteer who makes the call records the data on a standardized form and you therefore complete your records in a consistent way. The volunteer receiving the call is reminded that you are, in fact, monitoring his/her progress and has the added benefit of human contact with your office—since off-site volunteers can often feel isolated. (Again, see the end of this chapter for tips on using e-mail to get data from off-site volunteers.)

Another consideration, especially with volunteers working in the field, is to question the value of trying to record specific hours and minutes (i.e., I started at 5:13 and ended at 6:27). Instead, determine legitimate average amounts of time for ongoing tasks: the number of hours it usually takes to prepare for and coach a basketball game, the number of minutes usually spent in delivering a hot meal to a homebound person, the number of hours in an average tutoring session. You can develop these estimates by keeping extremely detailed records for a period of, perhaps, two months. When you have gathered actual times for this duration, you can then extrapolate the data to the rest of the year.

Using the average time estimates, from then on volunteers need only record the number of *activities* they have completed (i.e., number of games coached, number of meals delivered, number of tutoring sessions) in that month. When you receive their reports on the units of activities, *you* multiply these times the hour estimates you have established. Then you can report the "estimated total hours contributed" with a high degree of accuracy.

As with all averages, it is true that some games or visits will be longer and others shorter than usual. But over time these will balance out. If a volunteer has spent an exceptionally long time on a particular activity, s/he can certainly report this to you for inclusion in the statistics.

VOLUNTEER PROGRESS/ACTIVITY REPORTS

Concern for accountability has caused some volunteer programs to require detailed reports from volunteers describing all their activities. This paperwork is appropriate when such reports are actually read and *used*. For example, if a volunteer's report becomes part of a client's file as a supplement to other staff reports, then you are justified in asking for details. However, all too often volunteer reports accumulate in a file cabinet and serve no real purpose.

Before you invent another form, examine your timekeeping system to see if you can incorporate simple and efficient activity reports without burdening volunteers with paperwork. For example, we have already suggested (page 20) that individual timesheets could include a column for daily *highlights* of a volunteer's activity.

To insure that you receive accurate and complete reports (if you do decide to require them), be sure that volunteers understand the rationale for this task. They should feel that their reports are an important part of their overall contribution to the agency or organization. If you are introducing a new report form, or making changes in your recordkeeping system that will require more work for volunteers, be sure to involve volunteers in all stages of the process. After all, who is better able to tell you how hard or easy the form is to complete than the very people who will be asked to use it? Also, volunteers may come up with some creative and easy ways of gathering the data.

Some volunteers may balk at submitting reports about their contact with clients if they feel that their relationship should be a confidential one. One approach is to design a report form that can be completed by the volunteer and the client *together* —sort of a "diary" of their shared time.

RECORDS ABOUT GROUP VOLUNTEERING

The parts of the core system just described are for keeping track of individual volunteers. However, you may also be working with community groups, school classes, or other organizations that provide you with the time and services of their members.

A good software program will allow you to create a separate file area for group sources of volunteers. At a minimum, you will want to be able to enter and retrieve information on the name of the group, mailing address, telephone and fax numbers, and a short description. You will also need fields for current contact person, position with the group, and where/how that individual can be reached (which may well be different from the group itself, especially if new volunteers are elected into officer positions on a regular basis). Then you want to be able to record the service record of the group: dates and types of ongoing assignments carried or special projects completed, and any other management data you will need to work with the group.

Make sure that the individual Volunteer Data Records can be linked to groups as necessary. Either by entering the group name or an assigned code into the individual record, the computer ought to be able to give you a report of which volunteers are part of which groups. It's also very useful to be able to work from both directions: when you are in the Volunteer Data Record, you want to see group affiliation; when you are in the Group Record, you want to be able to see a list of members who are volunteers.

Create a folder for each sponsor organization and keep these folders in a special section of your file. Each folder can then store all correspondence and other records related to the group.

Your recordkeeping procedure will be determined by the way in which volunteers come to you from the sponsor organization:

Assigned to You Regularly: If volunteers from the group are assigned to you on a regular basis, you can incorporate them into your usual recordkeeping system as individuals, noting in their individual Volunteer Data Records that they come via a particular sponsoring group.

Sent for Special Projects: If the sponsor is sending a group of volunteers to handle a one-shot project, such as a party, you need a method to document the number of people involved and the amount and type of involvement. Therefore, you can develop a *Special Projects Report* that can be completed on the day of the event. At the top of the form, provide space for date, name of sponsor group, type of activity, and other identifying information. Then provide lines for each participating volunteer to sign in (which documents the names of everyone involved for insurance purposes and also for later recognition/thanks by you). If you expect to send personal notes of appreciation, have each volunteer also give you his/her address on the form.

If the participating volunteers are all coming and leaving at the same time, you can simply note the number of hours the activity took and multiply that times the number of volunteers to determine the total contribution of time for that event. If each volunteer serves on a different schedule or spent a different amount of time preparing for the event, make a column for "hours" and have each person note her or his personal total on the line with name and address. Then you can add up the column to calculate the grand total of hours contributed.

Note the name of the leader of the group and ask her or him to initial the form, verifying that it shows the names of all participants, before submitting it to you. Special Project Reports should be filed in the manner most useful to you:

- ☐ If you want a history of that group's involvement, file their reports in the group's folder.
- ☐ If you want a yearly record of all group projects regardless of sponsor, file all reports into a yearly "Special Projects" folder.
- ☐ If you want a monthly compilation of all volunteer activity, both individual and group, file the Special Projects Reports in the monthly folders with the Individual Time Reports.

You can cross-reference information as necessary. Remember to pick up the tally of hours served from the Special Projects Reports when compiling and reporting your grand totals of all volunteer activity.

See the next page for a sample Special Project/Group Sign-In Sheet.

Group Sign-In

Organization Name	Project		Date

Participant Names and Addresses	Task Assigned	Hours
Group Representative:	Total # of Volunteers: Total Hours:	

HARD-TO-TRACK DATA

Your volunteer program may benefit from some types of volunteer services that are difficult to document—yet should be reported and recognized in some way. Some examples are:

- The time spent by members of the Board of Directors (who are also volunteers)
- The work various committee members do in-between meetings
- The contribution of "on call," standby volunteers
- The involvement by clients of your organization as participants in self-help efforts or in running a special event
- The time spent by any volunteer preparing for an on-site assignment

These sorts of contributions are often invisible to the organization even though they are critical to the success of programs.

You might develop a quarterly report form (paper or electronic) to "capture" this sort of contributed service, giving people the opportunity to tell you what they have been doing on your behalf that has not been documented elsewhere.

MEANINGFUL DATA

Whether or not you collect and report on hours contributed by volunteers, remember that the only valid indicator of the *impact* of volunteer service is the quantity and quality of *work performed*. Therefore, you always want to keep data on *what* volunteers do as well as on *how long* it takes them to do it: number of patients visited, number of children tutored, number and variety of special entertainment provided, etc.

If you can report on "benchmarks" achieved, you will do even more to show the value of volunteers. For example, how many students have moved to a higher reading level as a result of volunteer tutoring sessions? How many probationers have improved their school or work attendance since being matched with a volunteer? What percentage of residents now attend the weekly exercise class as compared to before the volunteers accompanied them? This type of information will not only mean something to your administration, it will be important recognition to volunteers themselves.

Because all organizations are different, you will have to determine what data you need to collect and the best ways to do so. Just remember that this is tied to the annual goals and objectives of the volunteer program. The sequence must go like this:

First: Articulate what you expect volunteers to accomplish in X time.
Next: Determine what information will help you assess what is being done and how well.
Then: Develop a system to gather and record this information.
Finally: At the end of X period of time, tally the data and assess it.

OTHER PROGRAM RECORDS

Though the core system just described provides a great deal of valuable information, it still may not answer all of *your* management questions. Most volunteer programs have additional recordkeeping needs unique to their function or structure. In planning the forms to complete your system, be sure you know why you are gathering any additional data and *how* you will use what you collect.

The work that you, as program leader, do is also worthy of recording and reporting. Here are two types of data tracking procedures to consider.

Volunteer Program Manager's Log

Keeping a personal log of your own activities as volunteer program manager can be very helpful in managing your time, documenting the work that you do in coordinating the program, and juggling the details of the job. Some people use their appointment calendars to record their activities in diary form. This method works to a certain degree, but it is difficult to retrieve specific information without having to weed through random notes on each page. On the other hand, as personal electronic notepads become more sophisticated, it will become easy to use them not only to do scheduling and make notes to yourself, but also to search for information and create reports from what you've recorded.

In the absence of a Palm Pilot™ or similar device, you can create a useful personal logging system by recording your various tasks either in an electronic spreadsheet such as Microsoft Excel™ or in a paper notebook kept close at hand on your desk. Pages are divided into columns or the spreadsheet has its fields—as many as you need to cover all the types of activities you perform. For example:

Date	Telephone Calls	Letters	Prospective Volunteer Interview	Meetings	Expenses	(etc.) →→

Some of the columns record data that you may not be capturing elsewhere. For example, by listing all prospective volunteers you interview, you have a monthly total of your screening efforts that documents how many people were screened out as well as how many were eventually accepted. Here is also where you can record your speaking engagements and other time-consuming activities that should be included in your monthly report (see page 45).

Use whatever abbreviations mean something to you, e.g., "t" and "f" work well for "to" and "from" under the telephone and correspondence columns. At the end of each day, draw a line horizontally across the page and you are ready to start again. This means you keep working down the page and through the notebook, producing a continuous record.

Initially it will take a conscious effort to remember to jot down everything you do, but before long it will become second nature. And you will be surprised at how often you refer to previous entries.

Requests for Service Log

Volunteer departments are often the "chief cooks and bottle washers" of their organizations. During the course of a year, you probably receive quite a number of requests to provide volunteer help for unusual projects, large and small. All too often, such requests and your helpful responses are not recorded anywhere, so volunteer time, effort and service are soon forgotten. By keeping track of requests for assistance, you will be able to demonstrate the full extent of volunteer contributions to your organization.

A simple way to do this is once again to use either a dedicated database or a paper log book with columns, such as the one on the next page. Obviously you can adapt this sort of a log to your needs, and after a period of time you will have quite a record of such things as: tours conducted, mass mailings handled, escort services provided, Halloween pumpkins carved, special client needs met, etc.

You can add a column or field for "time spent," in which you record the amount of time you and/or volunteers needed to accomplish the requested task. The "date completed" column keeps you aware of any requests that are still pending resolution.

Enter all requests received into the log, even those you are unable to handle or decide not to handle. Include your reasons for saying no in the "comments" column. In this way, you will document inappropriate requests (their sources, frequency, etc.) and be able to show that you respond consistently in a helpful way to appropriate requests.

This log should be used for requests from sources outside your organization, as well as from in-house staff, so you can record the variety of ways you are called upon to help other volunteer programs, referring agencies, the press, etc. Over the course of several months, such data can help you prove the volunteer program's role in the community. On the other hand, when you review the in-house sources of requests, you will gain specific information about exactly who does and does not utilize volunteer services.

If you receive a great number of requests, or operate something like an information and referral project, you can increase the usefulness of this system by adding one other component: a request *form*. This form is where you can note all the details of the request and how you handled it. It can be completed by the requester or by you while you speak to the requester on the phone. This can also be done by electronic form.

Requests for Service Log

Date Rec'd	Source	Type of Request	Handled by & comments	Date Comp.

Number each form consecutively as it comes in, noting the number in the log, next to date. This is the sort of thing that a database program will do for you automatically. Then file all completed forms *numerically* in your file cabinet. This makes it easy to use the log as an index to your completed forms and to refer back to previous requests.

One of the most satisfying ways to use the data in the Requests for Service Log is at the annual volunteer recognition event. Think about how good volunteers will feel when you are able to thank them not only for fulfilling their regular assignment, but also for giving a special tour on quick notice to those visitors from Kenya! Now *that's* recognition.

E-MAILING REPORTS

As time goes on and more and more volunteers have e-mail, you will find yourself using electronic data gathering all the time[1]. All of the suggestions given here for how to design and format a paper reporting system apply equally to e-mail, whether you ask volunteers to enter data within the text of the e-mail or on an electronic attachment. Here are some specific suggestions:

 ☞ Create a separate mailbox and e-mail address specifically for volunteer reports. For example: reports@agency.org or keepingtrack@agency.org. This will free your main mailbox for other messages and will allow you to set aside time to focus on all the records-related messages in the other box. It also leads to another volunteer assignment: e-mail opener! By segregating the e-mails related to statistics and reports, you can train an interested volunteer to read them, collate the data, deal with standard inquiries, and alert you to items needing your attention. (See the section on "Cyber Deputies" in the next chapter.)

🖐 Create an electronic report "form" with consistent, key questions. Train volunteers to expect an e-mail with this form on a bi-weekly or monthly basis. Follow up if you do not receive a response within 48 hours. Rather than seeming like nagging, this shows the volunteer that you are paying attention and that progress on this assignment is important.

🖐 Ask volunteers to include a few sentences about "What my next steps will be" whenever they send you a report or an interim work product.

It takes some attention to use e-mail effectively. Send brief messages and be clear about what action, if any, is needed and by when. Use the message bar to your advantage. When people receive a ton of e-mail, they scroll down their mailbox and use the message bars to prioritize what they will read. Develop a standard message bar vocabulary and encourage everyone to get into the habit of using it. For example:

🖐 First, decide on an acronym for the volunteer program and use it as the first item consistently. So, the Hometown Tutoring Service might become: "HTS."

🖐 When you send a regularly-scheduled report form, you might say:
   "HTS: Please report now for <date period>"

🖐 For general information e-mails, the message bar might say:
   "HTS INFO: <subject><date>"

🖐 If you need a response quickly, you might say:
   "HTS: RESPONSE NEEDED A.S.A.P.!"

This will also allow volunteers to save important e-mails in computer files matching the message bars—which means that everyone will be storing them in the same way. For committees or boards of directors using e-mail communication, this can be a very useful way to systemize files.

Note, of course, that these tips on using e-mail effectively work in reverse, too. Teach volunteers to alert you in the message bar of e-mails when they need *you* to respond in order to move work forward.

The key is to track responses. If you send out e-mails and never follow up with those who do not answer your questions, word will soon get out that you are not serious about monitoring the program. Speak to your agency's Webmaster or Internet Service Provider and see if you can create automatic response devices that acknowledge receipt of e-mail and generate reports to you.

---

[1]For more information about communicating online, whether in working with volunteers in virtual assignments or simply e-mailing to any volunteer, see *The Virtual Volunteering Guidebook: How to Apply the Principles of Real-World Volunteer Management to Online Service*, by Susan J. Ellis and Jayne Cravens (Impact Online: 2000), which is available as a free electronic publication at: http://www.energizeinc.com/download/vvguide.pdf

4 Design, Management and Upkeep

It is a continuous activity to keep your recordkeeping system current and useful. Here are some guidelines to help you make the right decisions in each of the areas that are crucial to maintenance of your system.

DESIGNING FORMS

The heart of every recordkeeping system is forms. Your program needs and objectives should govern what forms are developed, which in turn generate procedures, data, and records. Good forms end up saving time, not wasting it.

Even if you are fully computerized, you will still need some paper forms. In fact, if you do not design forms to gather the data you need, the computer software will be useless to you.

Format

Select the format for each of your forms that will maximize its use. Ask yourself: Will this form be kept as a record or will the information be transferred onto something else? Is this form only for in-house purposes or will it be seen by many others? How and where will it be kept? How often will it be referred to?

A good recordkeeping system involves a creative combination of formats appropriate to the varied purposes of forms. Format options include:

Paper:
- Use inexpensive, low-quality paper for forms that are in-house and temporary.
- Use paper of greater weight and quality for forms that are permanent records.
- Use half-sheets or third-sheets if that is all you need.
- Keep size uniform if the form is part of a series of related forms.
- For a long form, consider the pros and cons of printing on both sides of the paper vs. using two separate pages stapled together.

Card Stock:
- Use card stock (index card weight) instead of paper when the form contains information that is needed often and therefore will be handled frequently. Cards wear better than paper.
- Index cards are easy to count and to group into special clusters of information when necessary.

- All the standard sizes of index cards have matching table-top storage boxes. This allows information on index cards to be kept at your fingertips.
- Select the size card that adequately accommodates the quantity of information.
- Be aware that a common mistake is to include more information on a card than is needed, thus making the card crowded and hard to read.

Storage options include file folders and looseleaf/binder notebooks.

E-forms:

If the items above sound quaint to you, here are some considerations for designing electronic forms:

- E-mail can be read by any computer system, so it may be best to create e-mails in which the form is part of the text. That way, a volunteer can fill in the blanks, hit "send" and return it to you.
- If you create forms as documents in a word processing program and send them as attachments to e-mail, be prepared that not everyone will a) know how to open and use attachments, and b) be able to read your document on their operating or word processing system.
- The hints below for "order" are equally valid even with an e-mail form.

Order

As important as your content is the way in which you order the information requested. Too many forms are a jumble of questions that skip from subject to subject. Consider the following:

- Follow a logical sequence of questions, grouping related items together.
- Place important information near the top of the form, working your way to the bottom or to the other side with secondary information.
- Leave sufficient space for data to be entered.
- Vary the way in which you ask for information, especially in order to save time and effort in completing the form. Columns and boxes to check off are very useful for this purpose.

Color

Color is a wonderful tool for recordkeeping systems, provided that it is used sparingly and consistently. The major purposes of using color are: quick recognition of material; easy retrievability; and to make a particular form distinctive or noticeable.

For example, if you want to differentiate a specific project, unit or aspect of your program, you could print all forms related to it in the same color. Or, you could color code an index file or folders to indicate particular age groups, sexes, geographic locations, assignment sites, or whatever subgroupings you most need to see at a glance.

But beware. Color coding stops being effective when no one can remember what the colors represent!

PRINTING FORMS

First, every new form should be pilot-tested before you pay good money to have it printed formally. Only once a form is actually in use can you be sure it is doing what you designed it to do. Most volunteer program recordkeeping systems do not require many printed forms; photocopied forms do just as well. However, all forms must be legible and add to the positive image of your program. Formal printing should be considered mainly for those forms seen by the public, such as volunteer application forms.

Second, *do not overprint*! After pilot testing a form and revising it if necessary, try to estimate the number of copies you will need in a year. Be conservative. It is better to reprint than to have out-of-date and unusable copies left over.

At the bottom of each form, note the date of printing and how many copies you made, e.g., "6/X1: 500." This will allow you to keep track of your needs for the form. A revision could then be noted: "Rev. 6/X2:500."

If your program has a logo, use it on those forms that will be seen by the public or even by other agency staff. This is another way of keeping your program visible and of making forms more pleasant to complete.

21st Century Update

Wasn't the previous material on printing funny to read? While everything is still valid for printing on paper, for the most part in today's world it is no longer necessary to pre-print most things. The beautiful thing about computers is that you can store any form you design and *print it out when you need it*. This also means that updating a form is a snap—and immediately ready for you to print and use.

DUPLICATION

Only when you examine the total picture can you recognize unnecessary duplication of information and ways in which you can eliminate forms and procedures. If a system is allowed to grow randomly, irrelevant information is often repeated, wasting time.

For example, it is common always to cluster "name, address and telephone number" and to repeat or transfer this complete cluster onto every form. But usually all you really need is the volunteer's *name*. As long as the main volunteer record contains all this information, it is rarely necessary to keep repeating it. If you duplicate the data, whenever a change of address occurs, corrections must be made in every place the original information appears! This is what makes recordkeeping tedious and boring.

Again, in the 21st century, the computer will assure that any address or other changes you enter in the main record will automatically appear throughout the entire database. This is another reason to stop asking people to fill in the same information over and over.

CONSOLIDATION

Duplication is relatively easy to recognize once the system is looked at as a whole, but the potential for consolidation may require more scrutiny. Ask yourself:

- ☑ Could additional questions, boxes to check, etc. be added to one form, thereby eliminating a second (or more) form(s)?
- ☑ Could printing a form in several colors eliminate the need for several versions of that form that differ now mainly in their headings?
- ☑ Could two, closely-related forms be completed simultaneously, thus easing collection efforts?

It is a challenge to find ways to streamline your system by effectively consolidating forms and procedures.

WASTE

Be honest: if you cannot think of a reason why you are collecting some piece of information—STOP DOING IT!

WHO DOES IT?

Clerical volunteers who enjoy the tasks of recordkeeping can be extremely helpful in collecting and tallying forms and statistical information on a regular basis. However, it is imperative that only one or two people handle the key tasks of logging and filing data. This assures consistent entries. Usually this would be the responsibility of the volunteer program manager and the volunteer program secretary.

A word to the wise: stay current with your recordkeeping tasks and they will not become unmanageable.

CYBER DEPUTIES

There are many people out there who enjoy both working with a computer and compiling data. Many volunteer program managers do not. So isn't it wonderful if you can recruit a volunteer who really likes to organize electronic files, freeing you of the technical tasks so you can concentrate on what information you need and how you need to use it? Several years ago a friend coined the term "cyber deputy" and it's been enjoyed ever since. The title "Cyber Deputy for Recordkeeping" is fun and attractive to the right person (who may, by the way, be a teenager!).

The tip just shared above applies for cyber deputies as well: limit the number of people who actually enter data into your system, so that you can assure consistency...and perhaps confidentiality, too.

FILING

A file cabinet can become a permanent wastebasket unless items stored in it are easily retrievable. You should organize your files in a way that fits your management needs. Just be sure that you (and anyone else who uses the file) are consistent in how items are placed, retrieved, and returned. Some points to consider are:

- *Eye-level:* Place often-needed files in upper file cabinet drawers, making them easier to use at a comfortable eye level.

- *Order:* Total alphabetical order is not the best way to arrange file folders. Consider the types of information you are storing in the file and determine useful "subject headings" under which you can cluster materials either alphabetically or chronologically. Use "file guides" (heavy cardboard dividers that are higher than the folders and therefore immediately visible) to label and separate the clusters.   Some subject headings you might want to use include: Active Volunteers; Inactive Volunteers; Sponsor Organizations; Annual Recognition Events; Special Projects; Monthly Reports; Media Contacts; Recruitment Efforts; Grants and Budgets; etc.

- *Correspondence:* Most correspondence should be filed in a specific folder relating to the subject of the letter or to the sender/recipient. Try to avoid "catch all" folders labeled simply "Correspondence 20X1." If you accumulate several pieces of paper related to the same subject, person, or project, make a special folder to hold them all. Only place "one-shot" items into a general miscellaneous correspondence folder.

- *Place Markers:* Whenever you or anyone else removes a folder from the file, insert a place marker strip in the vacant space. You can create such strips from cardboard or colored construction paper, cutting them to a size a bit higher than the file folders. Inserting a strip when removing a folder makes refiling quick and easy. If useful to you, create space on the marker for noting the date, time, and person removing the file folder. Keep a stack of the marker strips on top of the file cabinet for this purpose.

- *Inside the Folder:* Within each folder, arrange materials chronologically, with the most recent item on top. Staple or clip related items together, avoiding a folder filled with loose bits of data that fall out with use.

- *Labels:* The way you label each folder contributes to better use of the file system. Whenever possible type labels or at least print large and legibly. Labels should be placed consistently at the same location on each folder, though this can vary with each subject heading cluster. For example, all folders filed behind the file guide reading "Sponsor Organizations" might have their labels placed at the far right corner, while all folders under "Special Projects" might have labels at the far left corner. Within sections avoid "staggered" labeling, since it is easily disrupted when folders are added or deleted.

WEEDING AND UPDATING

One way to assure that your recordkeeping system remains meaningful as time goes on is to review each part of the system on a regular basis. Evaluate whether or not each form or procedure is still accomplishing what it was designed to do. If it is not, make revisions as necessary and *discard* or *discontinue* what is no longer useful.

To be sure that this important task is not overlooked, try scheduling an annual "Weeding Out Week" during which you examine your forms and go through your files for outdated material.

The question often arises as to how long you should retain information, especially on past volunteers. There are no set rules, but you might want to use five years as a guideline. This amount of time should be sufficient to enable you to produce documentation for any IRS audit or insurance question that might arise. For records older than five years, do what your space allows. If necessary, place older records into storage boxes and label the contents clearly.

Historical material about the volunteer program as a whole, especially items useful to future directors, should never be discarded.

GUIDELINES FOR FORMS USE

Every time you introduce a new or revised form, take the time to draw up an instruction sheet for its completion and use. Be sure that this instruction sheet is distributed to everyone who will be using the form. Even if the form is completely "in-house" or very simple, having an instruction sheet on file will be a great orientation tool for a new secretary or for your successor.

A sample copy of each form and the accompanying instruction sheets should be placed into a looseleaf notebook to produce a *forms manual*. Even if you revise or delete a form, leave the original in the manual and add the newer versions following it (or in front of it). This will provide you with a history of your recordkeeping system.

BACK UP YOUR DATA!

Enough cannot be said about making sure your computer data has been "backed up." *Back up your data regularly and often!!!* If something goes wrong with your computer equipment and you have a backup of your data, you will only lose the time that it takes to service the equipment. Otherwise, you will lose all of the time that you have invested and will have to re-enter the information.

Rotate several disks so that, in case something fails, you have serveral back-up copies. On a regular basis, take one of the back-up disks to a totally different office (or home). This provides safety in case of fire or theft of the computer.

5 Powerful Reporting

Now that you have a recordkeeping system that provides you with a continuous flow of valuable data, you can put it to work in support of volunteers. In fact, you have a responsibility to convey the progress and achievements of volunteers collectively, both to your organization's administration and to the volunteers themselves.

It does take time to write good monthly reports, but you will find that a well-designed recordkeeping system will almost write the report for you. A monthly report should include both statistics and a narrative—regardless of whether or not your superiors request it! If volunteers are truly having an impact, then there should be something to "proclaim" on a regular basis. And if you don't do it, who will?

REPORT STATISTICS

You can develop a statistical "cover sheet" to your monthly report that highlights such basic information as how many volunteers are actively fulfilling what assignments. And, wow, is a computer helpful with this! (See the Appendix for the old manual method of reporting statistics.)

Do *not* be lured into reporting a "lump sum" statistic such as Number of Volunteers this Month or Total Number of Hours Contributed. Such grand totals are almost meaningless to show the extent of volunteer service. By all means have these two pieces of information on the report cover sheet, but only as the actual bottom line of all the data that contributed to them. At a minimum, the statistical cover sheet should show:

- Every volunteer assignment, by title. If you are really that large, then at least list every different work area or unit in which volunteers are placed.
- The number of volunteers active in each category at the start of the period, the number who left during the period, the number who joined as new during the period, and the number "carried" to the next period.
- Note hours next to each category.
- Any special categories of volunteer service and data for those.

You could also show number of vacancies per assignment or note any units of the organization without any volunteers assigned. The absence of data can be revealing.

Such a data summary immediately shows the reader a number of things:

- "Movement" in each assignment: Which seem to be stable? Which have turnover? Which have fewer or more volunteers? All such information should lead to the most important question of all: Why? And that's how you and your executives can assess the program.

- Which units of the organization are fully engaged with volunteers—and which are not. (Why?)

- Are there some assignments in which a few people give a huge number of hours versus others in which many people give only a few hours each? (Is this acceptable?)

If there are any major changes in statistics, such as a large rise or fall in the number of volunteers in a given month or a given assignment, explain why in your narrative. Similarly, describe any new assignment added—or the reason for a deletion. The more explanation you can give about your statistics, the more they will accomplish for you.

If your program has several large components, you may want to give a statistical breakdown for each, using additional grids divided into appropriate columns. If volunteering by groups is a substantial part of your program, add a statistical report to document this.

As you decide which statistics to report, give your program—and yourself—credit for such data as:

- Number of interviews of prospective volunteers (which should be higher than the number who ended up joining, because you do screening)
- Number of tours or other community relations conducted by your office
- Number of requests from administration handled by volunteers
- Number and type of consultations given to salaried staff (such as department heads, the p.r. director, etc.)
- Number of times someone from the community called to ask you for information, help, to speak, etc.

Such data demonstrates the full range of a volunteer program's activities and shows what you do with your time. The fact that you screen adequately, represent the organization to the public, and assist many levels of staff, adds to the proof that you are an asset worth supporting.

VOLUNTEERS WITH MULTIPLE ASSIGNMENTS

As already mentioned, you will undoubtedly have some volunteers who carry more than one assignment. Managerially, it's important to be accurate in identifying who is doing what activity. However, it is also important not to "double count" such busy volunteers. This is why we recommended (page 14) being able to designate which of several assignments is that volunteer's primary one. It is under the primary assignment that each volunteer will be counted.

For example, someone may be a driver on Tuesdays and a receptionist on alternate Saturdays. In that case you arbitrarily decide on one role as primary. If you have a few volunteers who do regularly-scheduled work but are also on call for a Speakers Bureau presentation, it's clear that their regular assignments are their primary ones. Similarly, if you have a volunteer program Advisory Council, chances are that most of the members are primarily active in frontline volunteer roles.

Depending on your software's capability, you want to generate statistics that give the whole picture. Here is a sample of what the cover sheet to your monthly report might look like.

Assignment	# at start	# multiple	# new	# new mult.	# ended	# end mult.	# carried	# carried mult.	total hours
Case Aides	5	0	1		1		5		112
Receptionists	7	1	1		0		8	1	180
Drivers	6		0		1		5		18
Artists	1	1	0		0		1		2
Coaches	12		3		1		14		79
Buddies	16	0	4	1	6		14	1	192
Party Committee	4	3	0		0		4	3	12
Advisory Council		10		2		2		10	30
Speakers Bureau	3	2	1				4	2	3
TOTALS	54		10		9		55		628

For those interested only in the "bottom line," the Totals row reports that you started the month with 54 volunteers, added 10 new ones while 9 volunteers left, and therefore you are starting the next month with a total of 55 active volunteers. The "multiple" columns are not totaled, since these figures only matter across each row.

When you read row by row, you see activity within each assignment area. Here is where the "multiple" data comes into play. So, the report tells the reader:

✦ You started the month with 5 case aides, accepted a new one, said good bye to one, and carried the same total of 5 into the next month—but supervisors worked with 6 individual volunteers during the course of the month.

❧ You started with 8 receptionists, 7 of whom do the reception work as their primary role and one who does this as an additional role. (While it is true that this grid does not identify what this one "multiple" does as a primary responsibility, that can be answered quickly by going to the computer for more details. The key thing is that the report reader knows that +1 person is in the total volunteer count elsewhere.) You added yet another receptionist during the month and lost no one, so you are carrying 9 volunteers in this function into the next month: 8 plus one in a multiple role.

❧ Your Advisory Council is limited to members who are currently active volunteers in other assignments. Therefore, while you have the services of 10 Council members who met once for 3 hours (that's why 30 hours is shown on that line), the Council members themselves are all counted elsewhere on the grid.

Clearly this type of statistical report shows a great deal about the transitions within each assignment and is much more informative than simply knowing "54 volunteers started the month."

The Totals row also shows the complete tally of 628 hours of volunteer service contributed during the month. But see how much more useful that figure is when it's possible to see how those hours were spent. Not only can the reader see which assignments received the most intention, but it is also possible to understand which assignments are most labor intensive. For example, half the number of Receptionists worked almost the same number of hours as the Coaches did.

DOLLAR VALUE OF VOLUNTEERS

It is sometimes useful to convert the data on volunteer hours contributed into "dollars and cents" to give a different perspective on the value of such donated services. If you do this, avoid the inaccurate technique of using the minimum or median wage as a valuation of volunteer time. Almost all volunteer assignments would warrant a higher hourly salary on the open market than such low figures.

Instead, you want to develop a legitimate dollar equivalent for donated time— based on dollar figures that will vary with each volunteer assignment in your agency. Since employees are hired on a pay scale, it makes sense that volunteers also should be considered at different pay levels to match the various assignments they do.

For a complete discussion of the "true dollar value" of volunteers, see Chapter 11, "The Dollar Value of Volunteers," in *From the Top Down: The Executive Role in Volunteer Program Success, revised edition* by Susan J. Ellis (Energize, 1996).

REPORT NARRATIVE

Again, never submit statistics without a narrative that explains the overall context of the figures quoted. Narratives do not have to be lengthy, but they should adequately describe the highs and lows of the period covered. Some points to remember:

❧ The person reading your report does not necessarily understand the daily workings of the volunteer program. So assess everything you write in terms of its clarity. Being too brief or using in-house jargon may defeat your purpose. You can check your success at making your point by having an objective person read your narrative before you submit it.

♦ When reporting a special project do not assume that the reader recognizes why it is "newsworthy." Use the "so-what?" factor: make sure what you say has meaning beyond "this happened." Consider giving information such as: How many volunteers were involved? What types of volunteers (ages, backgrounds, etc.)? Has this been done before? Will it be done again? Who requested it? What is the expected outcome? Which agency staff have been involved?

♦ Give credit, by name, to volunteers and salaried staff who do an extra special job. This is real recognition and helps in your relationships with employees.

♦ Do not be afraid to admit problems, providing you explain them and describe your proposed plan of attack to solve them.

♦ Be alert to additional uses for your report. Some ideas include:

  ◇ Share with the volunteers (after all, it's their report!)
  ◇ Share with all department heads/board members
  ◇ Share with key community organizations
  ◇ Share with funding sources
  ◇ Send to the local newspaper
  ◇ Compile into an Annual Report

SAMPLE FORMAT

Of course there are many ways to compose a narrative report and you must pick the style most suited to you. As a guide, you might want to use the following three worksheet pages. Try your hand at writing paragraphs on the variety of subjects described. See if the final product succeeds in giving a full picture of volunteer activities during the month. Experiment with other ways of presenting program information.

VOLUNTEER PROGRAM MONTHLY REPORT NARRATIVE

(1)   _____ has been an exciting month for our Volunteer Program. During the past weeks, we launched: (*one or more new projects involving volunteers, or a special event, or a new recruiting campaign, etc.*)

(2)   As can be seen from our statistical summary on the cover sheet of this report, much activity occurred this month. Of special interest is: (*anything "out of the ordinary" such as a high number of new volunteers or volunteers leaving the program, or an explanation of a new volunteer position title/category*)

(3)   Last month, this report mentioned that a number of projects are being developed. All progressed further this month, especially:

(4)   Volunteers are initiating several ideas, still in the planning stages. These include: (*...and progress will be reported next month*)

(5)   Having highlighted the new things that are going on, we would like to note that the assignments and projects already underway continue to provide a high caliber of service to our consumers and agency. As an example:

(6)   Though things are generally moving along at a fine pace, the program is experiencing some difficulty with: (*brief description of a problem and why it is troublesome*)

To solve this problem, we intend to: (*outline a strategy, including help needed*)

(7)   The Volunteer Office provided orientation and training this month in a number of ways: (*summarize types, size of group, length of sessions, which staff were involved, etc.*)

Volunteer Program staff also benefited from participation in volunteerism training seminars this month: (*describe topics, sponsor, value to you*)

(8)   Our statistics document services to agency consumers, but this month we also responded to requests for assistance from agency staff. Such requests—and our method of help—included:

(9)   Program coordinators and volunteers were in touch with many community organizations and individuals this month. Some of our most productive contacts included:

(10)   (Other possible things to include in your narrative:)

- *publicity received during month*
- *appendix of unsolicited letters of thank you to the program*
- *information on your publications, such as a newsletter*
- *your interrelationship with the rest of staff such as serving on an agency committee*
- *results of any program evaluations*
- *needs assessments*
- *recognition received (awards, etc.)*

(11)   In looking ahead to next month, the Volunteer Program plans to concentrate on these major priority areas, and might need to call upon the resources of the agency in the following ways:

Enthusiastically submitted,

_____

Director of Volunteer Resources

6 Plunging In

If you are now brimming over with ideas about designing or redesigning your recordkeeping system, you may also be feeling somewhat overwhelmed at the size of the task. There are no real shortcuts, since this is a complex job in which details matter a great deal. But you can meet this challenge in a way that lets others share in the decision making and implementation.

POSSIBLE RESISTANCE

You may have to be prepared to encounter some resistance to initiating or changing a recordkeeping system, especially if you inherited your present data-gathering process from a predecessor. Anything that looks like more paperwork will be met, at best, skeptically. But if you can show the new system's benefits—and enforce the rules for submitting forms consistently with everyone—after a period of time resisters will either comply or leave. Keep in mind that a volunteer who does not want to tell you what s/he is doing may not be doing all that much!

Sometimes volunteers argue "I don't care about how many hours I work here" or "You don't need to count my time and thank me." One response is to point out that recordkeeping is important for the organization's sake (see page 1).

Keeping records is another way for volunteers to show their commitment to your organization. Such data actually increases the value of the volunteered service by providing concrete evidence of community support that can be used in various ways. So point out that filling in those forms is really a *form of contribution* to the cause.

GET HELP

One suggestion is to form a Records Review Committee (or a Records Development Committee, depending on your starting point) made up of experienced volunteers. Also consider salaried staff representatives (remember that secretaries can be very helpful in this area). The volunteer program secretary certainly should be on the Committee from the very beginning. The Committee's purpose is to examine your recordkeeping as a total system, evaluating each piece and offering suggestions for redesigning or streamlining. Additional input can be requested from anyone who actually fills out your forms.

Another suggestion is to declare a moratorium on regular work for one week, during which you and the Records Review Committee concentrate your efforts on making needed changes. The benefit of such a total immersion approach is that it allows you time to work with the entire system at once, rather than drawing out the process in bits and pieces over several months. It is also easier to "sell" your new forms and procedures as a complete and efficient *package*—a more effective way of introducing changes than coming out with something new every month. You can then even call a staff meeting to present and explain everything at once. If you do not yet have a forms manual, this approach obviously makes it simple to develop one in a relatively short amount of time.

Other Perspectives

When you meet or talk with other volunteer administrators, include recordkeeping as a subject for sharing. You will find that looking at many sample forms from a variety of organizations helps you crystallize your own needs.

CHECKLIST

As a final aid, here is a list of questions to be kept in mind by you and your Committee as you evaluate existing forms and make decisions about future ones. These questions review and summarize the mental process of forms development.

1.	Why do we need this form?
2.	Why did we select this format?
3.	How often is this form used?
4.	Who completes this form? Do they know how?
5.	What happens to the completed form?
6.	Where and how do we store this information?
7.	How often do we need to refer to the data?
8.	Who else needs access to this information? How often?
9.	How well does this form mesh with the rest of our record-keeping system?
10.	Does this form do what we want it to do?

Appendix A:
If you are still using paper…

The following is the material we wrote back in 1980 and revised in 1990, when the majority of volunteer programs were keeping records solely on paper. This system still works! And if you use it, it will be snap to switch to a computer database at some point in the future.

VOLUNTEER RECORD: PAPER SYSTEM
(For rationale, see Chapter 2)

Volunteer Fact Cards

This is an index card designed to give you quick reference to the most frequently-needed information about each volunteer. It is usually a 3" x 5" card and therefore can be kept within easy reach on a desk or cabinet. You should have the cards printed so that information can be transferred readily into the spaces provided, and so that the cards will look uniform, allowing information to be found in the same spot on each card. All the data on the Fact Card comes directly from the application form.

Regardless of how you arrange your form, the following are elements to include on a Fact Card:

Element	Considerations
(order)	Index cards are only partially visible unless removed from their storage box. This means that the most important information *to you* must be high up on the front of the card.
Name of Volunteer	This should be at the top of the card, last name first for alphabetical filing.
Assignment & Supervisor	This should also be at the top, perhaps in the right corner, opposite "name." Consider marking "assignment" in pencil, since it may change over time and your purpose for the Fact Card is to have *current* information. Or, leave enough room to add new assignments as they come along. This will avoid having to retype the entire card.

Element	Considerations
Address, Telephone Numbers, & E-mail Address	These are also important to have accessible, though you probably need the phone numbers more often than the address. Even if your records are not kept on a computer, it is likely you will communicate by e-mail, so include a space to record the e-mail address.
Emergency Contact	It would be important to have this at your finger-tips, but it is hardly used every day. So it can appear on the bottom or even the back of the card.
Schedule	Again, this is changeable and so should be marked in pencil.
(special uses)	Your program may require special uses of the Fact Cards that suggest additional information to be included. For example, daily or weekly telephone contacts might need to be recorded. In this case you might select a 5"x 8" or larger size card and print columns for "date," "response," etc. But only add such detail if it *really* contributes to the efficiency of your work.
(duplication)	A duplicate Fact Card might be useful for the volunteer's immediate supervisor to keep. Such a duplicate should be made at the same time as the original is made for your master file of cards.
(active/terminated)	The file box in which you store Fact Cards should be divided into an "active" and a "terminated" section, or "current" and "past." All cards should be filed *alphabetically* within the appropriate section. It is useful to keep the cards of volunteers who have left the program because you may need to contact them or they may someday "reactivate" themselves.
(special clusters)	This Fact Card file is meant to be a complete program record of all volunteers in alphabetical order. If you feel you *really* need to identify sub-groups of volunteers quickly (such as certain assignments, geographic regions, age groups, etc.), this can be done either by *color coding* or by making duplicate cards for storage in separate boxes. But for most programs the Master Log (see page 52) will meet these needs.

Volunteer Fact Card	
Name:	Assignment/Supervisor
Day Phone:	
Evening Phone:	
Address:	Schedule
E-mail:	
Starting Date:	Ending Date:
Emergency Contact:	

VOLUNTEER FOLDERS: PAPER SYSTEM

If you are tracking everything manually, then you will need to add a special form inside each Volunteer Folder. Inside the front cover, attach a form entitled something like "Individual Volunteer Work Record." Simply, this form should begin with "name" and then provide columns for "month," "assignment carried," and "total hours." Do not store volunteer time sheets (see page 20) in the Folder, but *do* enter the monthly total of hours served on this Work Record. You can use the Work Record to record and explain periods of "inactive" status, such as vacations or illness. You can also note date of and reasons for termination. Here is a sample format for you to adapt:

Individual Work Record			
Volunteer's Name:			
Month/Year	Assignments(s) Carried	Total Hours	Notes/Comments

TRACKING ASSIGNMENTS: PAPER SYSTEM

The following is the heart of the manual assignment tracking system.

Master Log

The Master Log is the most comprehensive and permanent record of your program. Yet it is simple to maintain and provides a wealth of management information.

The Master Log is a loose-leaf notebook. All pages follow the same format, but are divided into sections by *volunteer assignment category*. No matter how many assignments you have—or how few volunteers are handling each one—you must nevertheless make a section for each category. The Master Log is a *chronological* record of each assignment. Nothing within it is alphabetical—you have your Fact Cards and Volunteer Folders for that.

Each page in the Master Log is headed like this:

Master Log							
Volunteer Assignment: _____							
Name	**Age**	**Sex**	**Race**	**Start Date**	*Optional Columns*	**End Date**	**Com't**

The elements of each page, from right to left, include:

Element	Considerations
Name of Volunteer	It does not matter whether you write first name first or last name first. Remember this is not an alphabetical log.
Age, Sex, Race	One of the catch-22s of administration is that you are legally barred from using information about an applicant's age, sex or race as a screening device, but you are then asked questions by funding sources such as: "What is the racial distribution of your volunteers?" You are permitted to ask for such data once volunteers are *accepted* into the program. These columns in the Master Log, therefore, allow you to note such data *once* and in such a way as to provide cumulative program statistics.

Element	Considerations
Age	For age, if you have asked for a birthdate, enter the month and year in the Log. Do not enter the actual age today, since that will change as time progresses. Date of birth never changes. If you do not ask for date of birth, you still have a good sense of who falls into certain age ranges: high school, young adults, retired people, etc. So you can develop a *code* for your own use and exercise your best judgement in placing volunteers into appropriate categories. Then enter the code designation into the "age" column in the Master Log. Be sure to provide a *key* to your code in the front of the book.
Sex	Sex can be noted simply as F or M.
Race	Race can be coded as necessary, using letters such as: W(hite), B(lack), H(ispanic), A(sian), NA (Native American), etc.
Starting Date	Month, day and year—or just month and year, depending on your need. Since this Master Log is a permanent record and will cover all the years of your program activity, always note the year with any date entry.
(optional columns)	This Log must be useful to you. It should allow you to record major items that you wish to document either for management or reporting purposes. All other information will appear in the Volunteer Folder or elsewhere, so use additional columns in the Log. Some possible column headings to add might be: "orientation date," "uniform receipt date," milestones such as "100 hours served," etc. Use as many or as few columns as are applicable.
Ending Date	Month, day and year—or just month and year.

Element	Considerations
Commitment	If you noted the volunteer's original commitment of service time, you can very easily compare the ending date" with the "starting date" and assess whether or not the commitment was upheld. (In fact, you may want to use one of your optional columns to record the volunteer's initial commitment period right in the Log.) So, in the last column, you can place either a "✓" for a completed commitment, or a "+" for more time given, or a "−" for less time given. In this simple way, you can definitively report on your retention rate by going down this column and counting your checks and plus/minus signs.

Special Note: Despite all the debate about "successful" retention rates, the only really *measurable* and *meaningful* indicator of retention is whether a person remains as a volunteer for at least as long as s/he initially planned. This means that a person could indicate at the start the intention to volunteer for one month, do so and legitimately stop after that time. By using this "commitment" column, you can record that period of service as *fulfilled*, rather than having it look as if that volunteer dropped out unexpectedly. The Master Log will be an accurate reflection of the satisfaction of volunteers with their participation in the program. |

How to Use the Master Log

In the first week of April 20X1[1], you interview and accept a new volunteer, Ann Asset. She will be assigned as a Case Aide, but will begin in June and plans to work for three summer months. You hold her application, but do *not* begin the recordkeeping system for her yet.

---

[1]We are using the accounting textbook trick of 20X1, 20X2, etc. to indicate years in our examples. When we first wrote *Proof Positive* in 1980, the "Y2K Bug" issue was not even on the horizon for us. So, of course, all the dates were shown as 19X1, or shortened to 3/67. Today we understand the need to show the whole 4-digit year, whether 19X1 or 20X1. We have updated everything below, except for the birthdays which still show as 3/67—meaning, naturally, 1967.

In the second week of April, you interview and accept Matthew Motivated. He begins work as a Case Aide the following week. You make up a Fact Card and Volunteer Folder for him, with an additional Fact Card for his immediate supervisor. You open the Master Log to the section on Case Aides and enter him on the next available line:

Master Log

Volunteer Assignment: Case Aides

Name	Age	Sex	Race	Start Date	Optional Columns		End Date	Com't
Pearl Previous	3/22	F	B	1/20X1				
Eileen Early	1/50	F	H	2/20X1				
Matthew Motivated	*5/67*	*M*	*W*	*4/20X1*				

April is a big recruiting month for you and you add still another Case Aide, William Willing. (You also add other volunteers who accept different assignments and are therefore entered onto those designated Master Log pages.)

Master Log

Volunteer Assignment: Case Aides

Name	Age	Sex	Race	Start Date	Optional Columns		End Date	Com't
Pearl Previous	3/22	F	B	1/20X1				
Eileen Early	1/50	F	H	2/20X1				
Matthew Motivated	5/67	M	W	4/20X1				
William Willing	*2/21*	*M*	*NA*	*4/20X1*				

During May, you keep adding volunteers, but no new Case Aides. And then suddenly it's June. Ann Asset reports to work and you enter her accordingly.

Master Log **Volunteer Assignment:** Case Aides							
Name	**Age**	**Sex**	**Race**	**Start Date**	*Optional Columns*	**End Date**	**Com't**
Pearl Previous	3/22	F	B	1/20X1			
Eileen Early	1/50	F	H	2/20X1			
Matthew Motivated	5/67	M	W	4/20X1			
William Willing	2/21	M	NA	4/20X1			
Ann Asset	*3/58*	*F*	*H*	*6/20X1*			

By the end of the summer, your Case Aide list has grown nicely. By August 30, however, two volunteers have departed. One is Ann Asset who, as you remember, was only scheduled to work for the summer and therefore fulfilled her commitment. However, Sam Surprise got transferred in his salaried job and is moving out of state. He leaves unexpectedly after only one month of service. Your Master Log page will record all of this as follows:

Master Log **Volunteer Assignment:** Case Aides							
Name	**Age**	**Sex**	**Race**	**Start Date**	*Optional Columns*	**End Date**	**Com't**
Pearl Previous	3/22	F	B	1/20X1			
Eileen Early	1/50	F	H	2/20X1			
Matthew Motivated	5/67	M	W	4/20X1			
William Willing	2/21	M	NA	4/20X1			
Ann Asset	3/58	F	H	6/20X1		8/20X1	✓
Molly Mediocre	1/35	F	B	7/20X1			
Sam Surprise	8/63	M	W	7/20X1		8/20X1	–
Fred Fervent	9/37	M	A	8/20X1			

Use a yellow or other very light color "highlighter" marker and *cross through the entire line* of those volunteers who have terminated. In this way, you can tell at a glance who is active, and who has left. Yet the information remains readable and part of the overall historical record of that assignment.

There are three common contingencies that the Master Log system accommodates:

1. Volunteers who hold more than one assignment

2. Volunteers who transfer assignments

3. Volunteers who reactivate after a previous termination

(1) More Than One Assignment: One of the problems of systems that do not break down data assignment-by-assignment is that volunteers who handle several responsibilities at the same time often do not get credit for them. Also, it is easy to forget the extra hands that kept a certain project going during a peak period. The Master Log avoids this by legitimately documenting the complete involvement of each volunteer.

Begin by determining the "primary" role of the volunteer, either based on the assignment receiving the greatest proportion of hours served or arbitrarily. For example, Tillie Talent is a Case Aide who occasionally does art work. You therefore consider "Case Aide" as her primary assignment and "Artist" as her additional assignment. The Case Aide page in the Master Log would look like this:

Master Log

Volunteer Assignment: Case Aides

Name	Age	Sex	Race	Start Date	Optional Columns		End Date	Com't
Pearl Previous	3/22	F	B	1/20X1				
Eileen Early	1/50	F	H	2/20X1				
Matthew Motivated	5/67	M	W	4/20X1				
William Willing	2/21	M	NA	4/20X1				
Fred Fervent	9/37	M	A	8/20X1				
Tillie Talent (also Artist)	*6/67*	*F*	*W*	*9/20X1*				

On the page for Artists, Tillie is entered like this:

Master Log							
Volunteer Assignment: Artists							
Name	**Age**	**Sex**	**Race**	**Start Date**	*Optional Columns*	**End Date**	**Com't**
Art Nouveau	11/59	M	W	8/20X1			
Tillie Talent (P: Case Aide)	*6/67*	*F*	*W*	*9/20X1*			

The designation "P: Case Aide" tells you Tillie's *primary* assignment. In this way, Tillie is credited for two simultaneous assignments and you have an accurate count of how many Case Aides *and* how many Artists you have working. However, because of the two asterisks (**) preceding Tillie's name on the Artist page, you will not count her a second time in any *overall* volunteer count. She will be "picked up" when you count the Case Aide page.

(2) Transfers: Transfers are easy. Let's say Joe Jump begins work in September as a Case Aide, but in October decides he would rather be a Driver. On the Case Aide page in the Master Log, you enter this:

Master Log							
Volunteer Assignment: Case Aides							
Name	**Age**	**Sex**	**Race**	**Start Date**	*Optional Columns*	**End Date**	**Com't**
Pearl Previous	3/22	F	B	1/20X1			
Eileen Early	1/50	F	H	2/20X1			
Matthew Motivated	5/67	M	W	4/20X1			
William Willing	2/21	M	NA	4/20X1			
Fred Fervent	9/37	M	A	8/20X1			
Tillie Talent (also Artist)	*6/67*	*F*	*W*	*9/20X1*			
Joe Jump	*3/70*	*M*	*W*	*9/20X1*			*Transfer to Driver 10/20X1*

On the Driver page, you enter this:

Master Log **Volunteer Assignment:** Drivers							
Name	**Age**	**Sex**	**Race**	**Start Date**	*Optional Columns*	**End Date**	**Com't**
Bill Bass	4/51	M	W	7/20X1			
Kelly Carr	5/60	F	W	8/20X1			
Joe Jump	*3/70*	*M*	*W*	*Transfer from Case Aide 10/20X1*			

(3) Reactivated Volunteers: Also easy. Find the volunteer's name in the previous pages, noting his or her termination date. Re-enter the reactivated volunteer on the appropriate assignment page. Next to the new starting date, note: "Reactivated."

ADAPTING THE SYSTEM FOR YOU

The Master Log concept is very flexible and can be adapted to a variety of circumstances. For example, if you are coordinating a volunteer program with several building sites, you can create a separate Log for each location. If you need to track certain special categories of volunteers, such as student interns, court-referred, or work program/stipended, you can label a section of the Log for them. Similarly, create Log sections for your Advisory Council or for service on major committees.

Some programs find it helpful to assign each new volunteer a number that is then used for filing, computer entry, and statistical counting. Numbers are not reused when volunteers leave the program, so the digits keep ascending. If you have this sort of system, designate the *first* column in the Master Log for "number" and note it before each volunteer's name. When volunteers hold more than one assignment, their individual number is repeated on each Log page. If a volunteer re-activates, his/her original number is also reactivated.

The beauty of the Master Log is that simply by *counting* information in the columns, you can quickly and accurately answer a wide variety of questions about your program at any particular date in time.

To demonstrate how you do this, use the following pages to give it a try.

On the following two pages you will find the four Master Log sheets previously presented.

Pretend it is **October 31, 20X1**. (Happy Halloween!)

See if you can answer the questions below by carefully counting the columns of data given. The answers appear on **page 63**.

QUESTIONS

1. How many volunteers have been active with the program during 20X1?

2. How many volunteers have been with the program since it started in January?

3. How many volunteers began work during October 20X1?

4. How many Artists are there currently in the program?

5. How many Receptionists are there currently in the program?

6. How many volunteers terminated during October?

7. Of the three volunteers who terminated since January, how many maintained their initial commitment of service?

8. How many men and how many women have volunteered so far this year?

9. How many volunteers this year have been over the age of 60? (For this exercise, consider anyone born on or before 1940 to be 60+.)

10. How many volunteers are actively involved as of October 31?

Master Log — **Volunteer Assignment:** Artists							
Name	**Age**	**Sex**	**Race**	**Start Date**	*Optional Columns*	**End Date**	**Com't**
Art Nouveau	11/59	M	W	8/20X1			
Tillie Talent (P: Case Aide)	*6/67*	*F*	*W*	*9/20X1*			

Master Log — **Volunteer Assignment:** Case Aides							
Name	**Age**	**Sex**	**Race**	**Start Date**	*Optional Columns*	**End Date**	**Com't**
Pearl Previous	3/22	F	B	1/20X1			
Eileen Early	1/50	F	H	2/20X1			
Matthew Motivated	5/67	M	W	4/20X1			
William Willing	2/21	M	NA	4/20X1			
Ann Asset	3/58	F	H	6/20X1		8/20X1	✓
Molly Mediocre	1/35	F	B	7/20X1			
Debbie Duty	4/52	F	B	7/20X1			
Sam Surprise	8/63	M	W	7/20X1		8/20X1	–
Fred Fervent	9/37	M	A	8/20X1			
Tillie Talent (also Artist)	6/61	F	W	9/20X1			
Joe Jump	3/70	M	W	9/20X1		Transfer to Driver 10/20X1	

Master Log **Volunteer Assignment:** Drivers							
Name	**Age**	**Sex**	**Race**	**Start Date**	*Optional Columns*	**End Date**	**Com't**
Bill Bass	4/51	M	W	7/20X1			
Kelly Carr	5/60	F	W	8/20X1			
Joe Jump	*3/70*	*M*	*W*	*Transfer from Case Aide 10/20X1*			

Master Log **Volunteer Assignment:** Receptionists							
Name	**Age**	**Sex**	**Race**	**Start Date**	*Optional Columns*	**End Date**	**Com't**
Polly Polite	9/42	F	B	1/20X1			
Henry Hie	8/50	M	A	2/20X1		10/20X1	+
Doris Dorr	3/66	F	W	5/20X1			
Gail Grin	8/58	F	W	10/20X1			

ANSWERS

1. 18 (Remember: do not count Joe Jump or Tillie Talent twice)
2. 2
3. 1 (Joe Jump was transferred in October, but not newly added)
4. 2
5. 3
6. 1 (And 1 "transferred")
7. 2 (1 exactly and 1 more than originally committed)
8. 8 men, 10 women
9. 2
10. 15

How did you do? It becomes easier with practice. Obviously, what you just did with only four Master Log pages can work in exactly the same way for as many assignment categories and volunteers as you have.

On the next page is a blank Master Log form. We have left two blank columns for your optional use.

Master Log

Volunteer Assignment:_____

Name	Age	Sex	Race	Start Date		End Date	Com't

REPORTING: MANUAL TALLYING
(For rationale, see Chapter 5)

Report Statistics

Simply by counting the relevant columns in your Master Log, you can quickly complete a grid such as the one below.

Note how this system provides much more focused and valuable information—in an easy to read way—than something like one lump figure of "volunteers this month" or "total hours served." These two overall figures actually appear on the grid, in the lower right hand corner, but are fully substantiated by all the data in the entire grid. As a management tool, this proposed statistical report allows you to track patterns of recruitment and retention, as well as variations in the ratio of volunteers to hours served in each assignment.

Notice how this grid reports transfers and double assignments. The transfer shown (refer to Joe Jump on pages 58-59) affects only the assignment category totals, not the grand total of volunteers on board, which is unchanged by a transfer. Transfers are only reported in the month in which they occur; in subsequent months transfers are absorbed into the regular totals.

The double assignment (refer to Tillie Talent on pages 57-58) is a bit more complex and must be reported every month for as long as the multiple assignment continues. Here, Tillie Talent is actually counted within the totals for Case Aides. However, she also appears as the +1 in the Artists category. Reading across the Artists line, you can tell at a glance that the program benefits from 1+1, or 2 Artists. Nevertheless, the notation + 1 does not affect the grand total of volunteers on board (15), in which Tillie has already been legitimately counted once as a Case Aide.

OCTOBER 20X1

Volunteer Program Monthly Statistics					
Assignment	**Number at Start of Month**	**Number New This Month**	**Number Ended This Month**	**Number Carried To**	**Hours**
Case Aides	9	0	0+1transf	8	240
Artists	1+1	0	0	1+1	35
Receptionists	3	1	1	3	100
Drivers	2	0+1transf	0	3	48
Totals	**15**	**1**	**1**	**15**	**423**

Proof Positive   © 2003 Energize, Inc.

Appendix: If You Are Still Using Paper...

Index

A–Z

Activity reports, 19, 20, 23, 24
Application form, 5-10
Assignments, recording and searching, 14-5, 49, 52-64
Attendance sheets, 21-2
Collection systems, 21-3, 30-1
Color coding, 16, 34, 36, 50
Commitment, initial, 8, 14, 54
Computerization, 2-4, 11-3, 35, 38
Consolidation, 36
Cyber deputies, 36
Dollar value of volunteers, 42
Duplication, 36
E-mail addresses, collecting, 6
E-mailing reports, 18, 30-1
Estimating time, 21, 23
Fields, computer, 12-3
Filing tips, 16, 21, 24, 25, 30, 37-8, 50, 51
Forms, designing, 33-5, 48, 49-51
Forms, electronic, 34
Getting help with recordkeeping, 23, 30-1, 36, 42, 47-8
Group volunteering, 24-6
Hard-to-track data, 27
History, maintaining records on, 3, 15, 38
Hours served, *see* Time, records on
Individual time reports, 18-21
Individual work record, 51
Master log, 52-64
Milestones, tracking 13-4
Multiple assignments, 14, 15, 21, 40-2, 57-8
Off-site volunteers, 23
Printing forms, 35
Purpose of recordkeeping, 1-2, 19, 24, 27, 43, 47
Quantity vs. quality, 27
Recognition, tracking, 13, 25

Report narratives, 42-6
Reports, program, 39-46
Reports, volunteer activity, 19, 20, 23, 24
Resistance to recordkeeping, 24, 47
Retention, records about, 8, 14, 54
Searching data, 12-3
Sign-in sheets, 21-2, 25-6
Skills of volunteers, finding, 13
Software, selecting 2-3
Special service requests, 29-30
Statistical reporting, 39-42, 60-3, 65
Telephone, reporting by, 23
Time, records on, 17-23, 40, 42, 51
Transfers, 58-9
Volunteer assignment record, 14-5
Volunteer data record, 11-4
Volunteer fact cards, 49-51
Volunteer folders, 16, 51
Volunteer program manager's activities, recording, 28-30, 40, 45
Weeding and updating, 38

SAMPLE FORMS

Application Form, 9-10
Group Sign-In Sheet, 26
Individual Time Report, 20
Individual Work Record, 51
Master Log Assignment Page, 64
Monthly Report Narrative (sample format), 44-6
Monthly Time Grid, 22
Requests for Services Log, 30
Time/Activity Report, 20
Volunteer Fact Card, 51
Volunteer Program Manager's Log, 28

...*especially for leaders of volunteers*

Energize Web site
keeps you on the cutting edge!

Already a favorite site among Internet users interested in volunteer issues, the Energize Web site is continually updated to be useful. You'll find:

- The monthly "Hot Topic" by Energize President Susan Ellis on issues of timely interest to leaders of volunteers. You can join in the dialogue by posting your opinions.
- An entire library of articles on volunteer management.
- The Energize Online Bookstore, with over 80 titles in print and electronic form, offering the chance to sample excerpts from books on volunteer management.
- Helpful tips to use every day in working with volunteers.
- Up-to-the-minute information on key conference, events, and training workshops.
- A DOVIA Directory, and links to other volunteer-related Web sites.
- Quotes and parables illuminating volunteering.
- A Job Bank for finding and posting volunteer leadership positions.

Bookmark It!

Mark the Energize Web site as a "favorite" in your Web browser and return to Energize often.

http://www.energizeinc.com

Receive free e-mail updates about our Web site and publications!
Easy online sign-up at: http://energizeinc.com/fillin/email.html